ON BE[
a Dog with
a Bone

*never give up
on your dreams*

Peggy McColl

Foreword by Zelda

1 Stafford Road
Suite 312
Nepean, Ontario K2H 1B9
(613) 299-5722

ISBN 0-9730431-1-3
Printed and bound in Canada
©2003 Peggy McColl

Cartoons provided by Randy Glasbergen
Editing by Janet Shorten
Cover Design by Bymedia Design Group: Steve Brenninkmeyer,
Art Director, and Jenn Arnold, Graphic Designer
Production by Destinies Publishing
Text Design by Marie Tappin

Printing number 10 9 8 7 6 5 4 3 2 1
Printing by National Printers, Ottawa, Ontario

National Library of Canada Cataloguing in Publication

McColl, Peggy
   On being a dog with a bone / Peggy McColl ; editing by Janet
Shorten.

ISBN 0-9730431-1-3

   1. Self-actualization (Psychology) I. Shorten, Janet II. Title.

BF637.S4M17 2003   158.1   C2003-900752-9

Dedication

To my sister Judy who reminds me to never
give up

Acknowledgments

Thank you to my wonderful son Michel for your wisdom and insight to include humor and stories in this book. There are many things that I truly love about you and words on a page could never express them fully. I do love your unconditional love for animals, especially dogs.

With a heart filled with gratitude, thank you Mom & Dad for your unconditional love and loyalty and for bringing dogs into my life.

My greatest challenge to complete this book was the effort to keep this section at a reasonable length. It was a tremendous challenge because of the overwhelming amount of help and support that many people (and dogs) so generously provided to complete, enhance, complement, and improve upon the ideas, messages and general content.

Special thanks to my sister Judy for reviewing the entire book and to your partner Gerry O'Beirn. Thank you both for your wonderful feedback and ideas.

Thank you to...

An incredibly talented writer/author Caroline Pignat for your investment of time, energy and creativity.

Craig Senior for your willingness to help and for reviewing the entire book and providing valuable suggestions.

Janet Shorten, once again, for putting your heart and soul into this project. It was a great comfort knowing that the editing would be nothing less than your usual high-level standards.

Marie Tappin for your professionalism, creativity and the velocity at which you can so perfectly complete the type-setting and text design.

Kevin Lauzon from National Printers for your profession-alism and your outstanding level of customer service.

Gail Baird for having faith in this book, in the messages and in me. Your knowledge of the book industry is warmly appreciated.

Melanie Rogers for providing the humorous quotations.

Deneen Newport for your inspiring story about Keaton.

Elizabeth Bennett & Robert Bennett for sharing your beautiful Charlie with the world (Charlie is the Bulldog on the cover of this book).

A sweet, giving, inspiring lady, Carol Gardner, and Zelda for writing a magical Foreword for this book.

Randy Glasbergen for allowing me to share in your wonderful talent with the cartoons that we have included in this book.

David Booth for investing the time with me to share in the wonderful stories of Max.

Dottie Walters, Dr. Paul Hartunian, Mark Victor Hansen, Bob Proctor, Joe Vitale and Linda Hines for providing your endorsement for this book. Your thoughtfulness is gratefully appreciated.

Steve Brenninkmeyer and Jenn Arnold for the cover design for this book and for doing a magnificent job, and for exceeding my expectations.

My Aunt Betty and Cousin Fern for sharing your stories that have also been included.

My business partner Debbie Heika for your unending support and friendship.

My wonderful dog-loving neighbor and friend Cheryl for your thoughtfulness and your constant generosity.

A special thanks to my incredible friends who support me every day in every way:

Bryon & Suzanne Petti, Fernando Martinez, Diane Craig, Anick Lavoie, Judith Yaworsky, Jerry Jenkins, Jane Pick, Colleen Moore & Barry Doucette, Brenda & Tom Moss, Denise Reid, Renée Fournier & Marc Desmarais, Trudy Marschall, Gina Hayden, Gilla Assaad, Fady Assaad, The Lessard Family (Christian, Maryse, Simon, Valerie, & Stephanie), Joe Vitale, David Riklan, Bradley Dugdale and Jack Canfield.

A big "woof" of thanks to all of the dogs that generously, unconditionally and willingly teach us humans some extremely valuable life lessons. A special thanks to:

Dee Dee, Noelle, Charlie, Max, Mack, Holly, Heidi, Nellie, Keaton and Zelda.

Table of Contents

Foreword by Zelda

You never know how tough you are until someone takes your bone away!

Leave it to a bulldog, me, to write the foreword to Peggy McColl's newest book, *On Being a Dog with a Bone*. After all, we bulldogs are born and bred with dogged determination in our genes. Have you ever noticed how our noses are slanted backwards so we can breathe without letting go of that bone?

In her book Peggy McColl explains how you can follow some doggone good guidelines to not only succeed but also to simplify your life. As a matter of fact, I wish I had read her book a few years back as I was starting my business, Zelda Wisdom, Inc. I chased my tail, I ingested things that weren't good for me, and I spent a lot of time in the dog house. Life is "ruff" and barking up the wrong trees instead of using my instincts to reach my goals didn't help. Once I found my 'bone," however, success came quickly.

On Being a Dog with a Bone briefly defines how you can learn some helpful tricks from man's best friends. I particuarly liked Peggy's concept of "drool unto others as you would want drooled unto you." I keep that message taped above my dog bowl.

The book will keep you thinking and smiling at the same time. Best of all, this book WILL teach you the tricks you need to reach your goals, to follow your dreams, and to succeed when you didn't think you could. Success comes when you can hang on after others let go. So, GO FOR IT!

Zelda

Introduction

Everyone has a desire to discover the great secrets of success, to reach total contentment, and to find the path to personal fulfillment. For centuries, we have turned to wise men and wise women for guidance. We would climb to the hermit's highest cave, we would trek through the desert, and we would scour the self-help section in bookstores for hours in our endless search for answers. But after all of this time, is it possible we may have been looking in the wrong places?

The wisdom we seek is not something that is out in the world. Everything you need is right here. Maybe all you needed to do was notice it. Don't look up, or out, or in; instead, look down. All the inspiration and insight you need is curled up at your feet.

Why do you suppose we call them man's best friend? Not only are dogs great friends; they have the potential to teach us some of life's most valuable lessons.

Anyone who has a dog knows that. But the lessons they share are not just for dog lovers.

Imagine what kind of world we would live in if all people shared the same high level of commitment, unconditional love, deep devotion and true loyalty of dogs. Imagine if everyone trusted and followed their instincts. Imagine a world where everyone reveled in the simple pleasures of life: running freely in an open field, driving down the country road with your head stuck out the window and the wind blowing through your hair, accepting the warm invitation to take a walk with a friend, or playing happily for hours without ever showing signs of fatigue. Yes, we have a lot to learn from our wise four-legged friends.

What about you? Are you feeling restless and unsatisfied? Are you ready to trust and to courageously step out . . . one paw at a time?

The answers you seek can be found within the pages of this book, and they aren't complicated. In fact, the key to success and happiness is quite simple. Let's get started by taking on the role of a dog with a bone and capture the essence of one of the most powerful keys to success: dogged determination.

Your guide dog to the pathway of your dreams is waiting for you. This book is your guide. Come for a journey with me and we'll dig up your dreams, sniff out your strengths, and roll in the bliss of success.

Remember – as you are reading, dog-ear the pages that have significant value and return to them later for inspiration and future reference.

Chapter 1

Dogged Determination
*Grab hold of that bone
and never let it go!*

Have you ever witnessed a dog with a bone? When a dog
has that bone in its mouth and someone attempts to grab
it, wiggle the bone, or pull on that bone to remove it, no
matter how hard they try, that doggie won't let go. As a
matter of fact, the harder they try, the deeper the dog will
sink its teeth. Now, that is sheer dogged determination, a
quality that is absolutely required if you want to achieve
any goal, no matter how large or small – regardless of the
size of the bone, or how large the dog is relative to the
size of the bone.

> *My only goal in life is to grow up to be the person
> that my dog thinks I am.*
> *~ Unknown ~*

If you know what you want

If you know what you want, and you want it unquestionably, become a dog with a bone. Clench your teeth firmly on that bone; don't let it go; be determined not to allow anyone or anything to take it from you.

There are all kinds of things in life that will try to yank that dream away from you: well-meaning loved ones, circumstances, unexpected events, other people's opinions, and possibly even your own doubts and fears. But that is exactly when you must clench your teeth and feel that surge of dogged determination.

You must be open and ready to receive new ideas and expand your present thought conditioning. You must be ready to let go of those "should haves" and "ought to's" and go after what you really want.

Challenge yourself to scratch out a new path and chase your dream. But be careful of the route you take. Take new paths. If you take the same route that you've been taking, you'll end up at the same destination. Is that where you desire to go?

Are you determined to live the life of your dreams? It's easy! Just decide.

If you don't know what you want

Begin by answering a few questions, such as: Is there something you have a burning desire to do? Is there something you've always dreamed of? What would you really like to have, do or be?

If the answer to one of these questions makes you feel excited, that feeling is passion. It's passion that ignites the determination to pursue the goal. Passion will keep your jaws clenched on that bone and not let it go.

If your dreams do not come from desire or from passion, it is less likely you'll maintain a high level of determination. You may have wondered why you haven't been able to stick to a goal; maybe you need to determine whether it is truly a desire, truly something that you are passionate about. If you are, great! Just ignite that passion once again and keep it going.

> *In order to keep an oil lamp lit, you must keep putting oil in it.*
> *~ Mother Teresa ~*

What if you don't have desire?

Determination is fueled by desire. If you display determination, whether for short periods or long periods, you do have desire. Desires can be short-lived or stay with you forever.

Short-lived desire is sometimes the result of a "be nice to have" thought. Deep desires come from the soul, and you'll recognize a deep desire simply by the way you feel about it in your heart.

> Be very careful what you set your heart upon, for you will surely have it.
> ~ Ralph Waldo Emerson ~

What does determination feel like?

When you have determination you feel an abundance of energy flowing through your body. This energy comes with a feeling of excitement. You start to feel as if you have more energy than you ever did before. Your ability to focus is intensified. You set your sights on a target and no matter what happens, you won't allow anything to take your eye off that goal.

Dogged determination means that you are holding onto your dream, tighter than ever. If someone tries to pry this dream away from you – it isn't going to happen. You take action toward its attainment every day and even though you don't know how you will achieve your goal, you keep going. When challenges come along you get excited because you know this is an opportunity to reveal the best of who you are, which is exactly what opportunities are designed to do.

When you have dogged determination you know that nothing is going to stop you. You become more energized, more determined, more persistent every day. You exude confidence, knowing that the outcome of your goal is absolutely certain and there is no other possible outcome. Being determined gives you an incredible natural high. You know that nothing will stop you and you show it in everything you do.

Being determined does not mean being without fear. You may feel fear, but because you are determined, you will move forward, take action, and be completely optimistic in spite of fear.

The following formula summarizes this well:

Desire + Focus + Courage = Determination

Start by knowing what you want

When you have a clear dream, that very moment, the magic seed is planted. From this seed, through your efforts of nurturing your goals and dreams with dogged determination, your goal will surely sprout and blossom.

If you researched the most accomplished people of our world, you'd find that they all had dogged determination. This is one quality possessed by all of these individuals.

Bones aren't delivered gift-wrapped

Dreams are not always obvious. Not everyone is aware of what their dreams are or what they want to do with their life. If you think someone is going to deliver a wonderful gift-wrapped bone, think again. You've got to be willing to go and dig for it. Sniff it out and start to dig.

Dogs will dig in many different places until they find that hidden bone. Your goals, your desires may be out there – or in there – waiting for you to find them. From time to time, your bone may show up for you and you'll know exactly what you want to do with your life. Or, you may not have a clear vision and need to dig some more. Don't stop digging until you uncover that dream.

Meet Max the Scotty

Max has a burning desire to play. Max's owner, David Booth, shared his story.

> *Max, born as Maximilion McDuff, is incorrigible. He loves to play; he loves everybody and everything. You start to throw the ball for him and he would literally keep going until his heart stopped. I think Max is a good example of full-steam playful, because if you are sitting there, he will persist.*
>
> *When we have guests over Max knows that he has a new mark. Max will go over and drop his toy at our guest's feet and he will keep doing it until they pick it up and throw it. He does not quit. He will keep at it until he gets his way.*

Max probably doesn't know the word "stop." Max removed this word from his recognition-vocabulary. He probably wouldn't listen anyway, and because of his determination he achieves what he desires.

Have you ever seen a human being behaving the same way? I have. I've seen incorrigible sales people. Even when you say, "no, thank you!" they keep selling. It is almost as if they don't hear the words. And if they keep asking in a style that is non-offensive, they likely do get the result they are striving for.

Max reminds us to keep going. He's cute and playful. He's not intrusive. He's not obnoxious. He simply has a desire to play, and he asks you to play with him. Sooner or later Max achieves the result that he intended. That is the power of dogged determination.

When you expand your thoughts from the dog with a desire to play, to a world champion athlete, a highly successful business person, a reformed addict, or even a young child with a desire to have a toy, you will find one key ingredient that keeps them committed to their goal. This one ingredient is determination, a.k.a. stick-to-it-iveness, tenacity or perseverance. Certainly world champion athletes, successful business people, and reformed addicts have their share of challenges, but despite challenges, they maintain their determination. In the face of adversity, they put themselves right back on track again.

Can you recognize determination?

For some this dogged determination may be a sleeping dog, lying dormant inside. These people have determination inside them, but they just don't express it. They have no drive, no focus and no direction for their life, and you'll recognize them by their lack of zest for life.

As for those truly inspired and determined people, you'll know them when you see them. Maybe you are one of them. Determination can be recognized immediately by high levels of enthusiasm and the impression of being unstoppable.

Everyone has determination within them. You can think of determination as energy within you. You have the ability to flip the switch and turn it on. You also have the ability to turn it off. You decide. Which do you choose?

One of my favorite movies is called *Rudy*. It's based on the true story of Daniel "Rudy" Reuttiger, who had a dream to play football for the University of Notre Dame football team. Rudy had some very real challenges to overcome.

Rudy was not very tall and had a relatively small frame. He was much smaller than the average football player and he did not have the grades to get into college. He was also dyslexic. His family and friends did not support his (as they called them) "stupid" dreams. They tried to convince him to let go of his dream, but Rudy was a dog with a bone and would not let go. He was determined to play football for Notre Dame, and he overcame every challenge until he truly did become a football player for the University of Notre Dame football team.

Rudy endured even when he felt very alone. He had a dream, he believed in himself, and he never lost sight of his goal. His commitment was tested from time to time, but despite feeling knocked down, he got right back up again and pushed harder.

Rudy became a role model for other Notre Dame football players. Perhaps Rudy is a role model for all of us.

Hold on to your values

Even though you need determination as you move toward your goal, it is equally important to keep in sight your most important values: health, honesty, integrity, family, friends, finances, or whatever the most important values are for you.

Being a dog with a bone does not mean that you take leave of your senses or lose your priorities. On the contrary, it is more important than ever to use your keen sense of logic, engage your common sense, and stay true to who you are and what is important to you.

Notice the effects of your determination and be aware if someone or something is suffering as a result, as I'm certain that would not be your intention. Give the things that matter to you in your life the attention they deserve, or they could potentially become a greater challenge down the road.

> *Get a good idea, work at it, stick with it, and dog it*
> *until it is done and done right.*
> *~ Walt Disney~*

Chapter 2

Time to Teach an Old Dog New Tricks
Learn the behaviors that will guarantee you success.

A dog teaches a boy fidelity, perseverance, and to turn around three times before lying down.
~ Robert Benchley ~

While I was writing this book, we added a new member to our family, Dee Dee. Dee Dee is a Shih Tzu puppy. As new puppy owners quickly find out, puppies don't come trained . . . at all. She didn't realize that she needed to do her "business" outside and not on our carpet or wherever she felt like doing it. We had to train her to go outside.

She also didn't know that she wasn't supposed to eat my slippers, chew on paper, scratch the walls, dig in the garden, eat the plants or bite our fingers. All of these things she needed to learn. And – here's the irony – telling her once didn't stop her from doing these things. We had to tell her over and over again.

We are very much like puppies. Our optimum time for training is when we are young, but how many people were trained to set and achieve goals by 2 years of age? How many people in their youth are taught the most effective methods of overcoming challenges and adversity? How many babies are taught the importance of a positive attitude before they start to walk?

As we get older, we start to realize that there might be more to life than what we are presently experiencing and we begin to have desires and dreams. But we might not have learned about pursuing our dreams, handling adversity and overcoming challenges at a young age. We must train or re-train ourselves with new disciplines. This can be time-consuming. Just like dogs, we are creatures of habit. We will continue to do the things we've always done unless we are trained to do otherwise.

Training a puppy in the early stages can be relatively quick, depending on your own commitment to the training and the dog's temperament. However, if you bring an older dog into your home, and it is not trained, the time it takes to train it can be considerably longer.

Several years ago my parents brought an older dog named Heidi into their home. Heidi is a Lhasa Apso. She was a neglected dog and was not properly trained as a puppy. My parents had to train Heidi as if she were a puppy to be housebroken. This was not an easy task, but they didn't give up. They were highly motivated to have their new pet housebroken. After a period of time –

longer than they would have liked – they succeeded in training Heidi.

At the time of writing this book Heidi was 14 years old, "old age" for a small dog. My mother told me that Heidi was reverting to her old behavior and was doing her "business" on the floor inside my parents' house. She said, "It's like training her all over again!"

Sometimes we, too, revert to our old behavior and have to train ourselves again. It's hard to imagine why we would ever go back to old self-limiting behaviors, but regardless of the reason, sometimes we do.

Training is like conditioning our own behaviors or disciplining ourselves to succeed. You can also think of it as building the muscles of discipline. Just as in building the physical muscles in our body, we have to constantly "go to the gym" to build up these muscles; otherwise we get out of condition. Our disciplines become "flabby" and our results will reflect this.

For dogs there is dog obedience school. In the past, when I visited a dog obedience school or a puppy training academy, I couldn't help but think of the similarities to continuing education. It is true that it is best to learn positive behavior at a young age, just like a puppy; however, we don't always receive the best training when we are in our youth. Therefore, commit yourself to an obedience school of personal growth.

How do I teach myself new tricks?

Once you know what you want to experience in your life, ask yourself this question: What skills, attributes, strengths, disciplines and characteristics do I need to develop and/or strengthen to achieve my goals? Make a list. Once you have your list, answer these questions: Where will I get the knowledge to develop these strengths? What will I do to develop these skills?

My belief is that we need to "go to school for the rest of our lives" – but not just any school. I'm referring to the school of life, the school of personal growth. This school is always open and the enrollment is available to anyone who chooses to enter. The only prerequisite is desire. When you have the desire and you add the determination, acquiring and applying the knowledge is going to be easier.

What do you want to do with your life? Once you know what you want, determine how you will learn the disciplines to help you succeed.

> *In order to really enjoy a dog, one doesn't merely try to train him to be semi-human. The point of it is to open oneself to the possibility of becoming partly a dog.*
> *~ Edward Hoagland ~*

Everyone has the ability to learn

If you think you can't learn, think again. One challenge people have is that they believe they cannot learn. For

27

example, beliefs such as "I'm too old to change now" is a limiting belief and will create barriers to learning new things. This type of belief must be replaced with a positive supportive belief: "I can learn anything when I commit to do so." Or "I am committed to learn whatever I need to know to achieve my goals."

Dogs don't doubt their ability to learn. If people believe that they cannot learn, they will not even attempt to learn. Believing that they do not have the ability to learn how to do something will stop them and hold them back from achievement.

If you have this belief, I strongly urge you to erase it from your mind and replace it with an open-minded belief. Commit yourself to learning new tricks, the tricks of success.

Maybe guidance is all you need

When your dog chews the remote control, or your slippers or books, or defecates on your carpet, maybe it is telling you that it hasn't had the guidance it needs! We humans, too, do things that are destructive, and we simply need to be reminded to change a behavioral pattern.

Maybe information is all you need

Does your dog ever tilt its head while you are talking to it? Do you suppose it simply doesn't understand? My belief is that the dog doesn't know what you are saying and is confused. I've never had a dog tell me otherwise.

When you are confused, it means that you may need to sniff out the answers or gather more information. Allow confusion to move you to gather the information you need to achieve the clarity you require.

Gaining clarity can be achieved in a number of ways. Asking questions is one of the best methods for acquiring knowledge. Be certain to ask the source or sources who are most qualified to provide you with the information you need. Invest the time and energy to research the knowledge that will lead you on the right path and be most beneficial to achieving your goals.

What are the disciplines that you need to succeed? Discover what these are for you. Commit to developing these success disciplines now and keep learning them until you master them.

"Right now I only have three bones, but I figure I'll need at least 750,000 bones when I retire."

Chapter 3

Don't Chase Your Tail
Stop doing things that get you nowhere.

When a man's best friend is his dog, that dog has a problem.
~ Edward Abbet ~

Why do dogs chase their tails? I don't believe there is a compelling reason for a dog to chase its tail, except that it doesn't realize what it is doing. Human beings are similar, and I know that because I've been there. No, I wasn't spinning in circles trying to bite my back pocket. I was doing things that got me nowhere, but not realizing it at the time.

Why do dogs turn around three times before they sit down? I was curious about this behavior, so I went looking for the answer. I read numerous books about the history of dogs. Apparently, the reason dogs turn around three times before they sit down, or lie down, is because they are preparing their bed. The dog actually descends from the wolf family, which lived in the wild and slept on branches and leaves. Turning around several times before lying down was for the purpose of stomping down the branches and leaves to create a more comfortable resting area.

A dog might chase its tail for no purpose. A dog turning around three times before lying down might have served an ancient purpose that is no longer relevant. After all, indoor dog beds are not usually made of branches and leaves.

We humans can learn from these two examples. First, we need to notice the things we do that waste time and get us nowhere. Second, we need to recognize if we are doing things that may have had a purpose in the past, but are not relevant to our goals today. If we notice ourselves doing them, we need to stop right away.

You may be familiar with this definition of insanity: "to do the same thing over and over and expect a different result." If your activities or behavior are not producing the results you desire, then be aware and evaluate these activities for effectiveness. If they add no value, stop doing them. It's as simple as that.

A friend of mine shared a story about her dog Nellie, a playful Border Collie. Even though Nellie wasn't an old dog, she had the characteristics of senility. When a guest arrived at their home and rang the doorbell at the front of the house, Nellie ran to the back door (where there wasn't a doorbell), barked and wagged her tail. Nellie thought the guest was arriving at the back door. Every time that doorbell rang, Nellie would bark, but sometimes at the front door and sometimes at the back door. Yet always the guest would enter through the front door.

It never did register with Nellie that the sound of the bell ringing indicated that someone was about to enter at the front of the house. Nellie simply didn't notice this pattern.

In addition, Nellie had a housemate pet named Baby. Baby was a Persian cat that loved to climb trees. Fortunately for Nellie and Baby, their yard was full of trees. Nellie often chased Baby around the yard until Baby got bored and climbed one of the trees. Nellie would stand at the base of the tree, head stretched upward, and bark. Sometimes Nellie sat at the base of a tree, stretched up her neck, and barked even though Baby was not in the tree. This made the owners laugh. Who knows why Nellie barked at the tree? Maybe there was a bird up there, or maybe she thought Baby had climbed up.

Are you barking up the wrong tree?

Humans are just like Nellie. In my career I've experienced similar scenarios, where I chased a lead or pursued a contact only to discover, after a tremendous amount of work, that they were not the right person in the first place, and I had wasted my time.

While Nellie barked up the wrong tree, if she had just looked at the other trees she might have found Baby sitting on a branch. When I looked at other contacts, I found the right one. A small shift in our focus can make the world of difference.

Our puppy Dee Dee loves to chase her ball. We'll throw the ball, Dee Dee will chase it, Dee Dee will bring it back to us, and we will repeat this process many times. Sometimes Dee Dee thinks the ball is under the sofa, when in fact it has rolled into the next room.

We laugh at the entertainment value of watching a dog think it is on target when it's very wide of the mark, but we do the same thing. We get fixated on one destination, but it's a dead end. If we shifted our direction by a fraction of a degree, we would be right on target.

Don't hurt yourself

There is potential pain in not realizing the results of your actions. Dee Dee, as a young puppy, loved to bite on electrical cords. If she continued, it could have led to extreme pain, or even death. She needed to learn not to bite into electrical wires. Similarly, we humans need to notice that if we keep doing some things that do not appear to hurt us now, we could be hurt if we keep going. What electrical cords are you biting?

Discover the things you did in the past that were time wasters, that prevented you from achieving your goal and may have even taken you in the opposite direction. This awareness will give you the wisdom to change or stop the previously harmful behavior.

As you move forward, heighten your awareness by noticing and recognizing other self-debilitating behaviors and stop those "getting nowhere" habits.

"I'm advertising my new business on the Web. For $25 an hour, I'll come to your house, lick your face, listen intently, wag my tail and be your best friend."

Chapter 4

Do Not Ingest Things That Are Not Good for You
Poisons sabotage success.

Ever notice that a dog only has two faces? The one you love, and the one you get as it sits and looks at you while it pees on your freshly washed floor!
~ Melanie Rogers ~

Have you ever seen a dog eat something that wasn't good for it? Our neighbor's otherwise well-fed dog Mack loves to eat insects. This is not pleasant to watch. Mack weighs only 3 pounds, and some of the insects he eats are about half his size. I don't think the nutritional value of the insects is worth the effect they have on his system. Sometimes when Mack eats these bugs, he gets very sick. Does he stop? No. He still insists on eating them.

As a little puppy, our dog Dee Dee chewed or ate everything she could get hold of. Because she was a puppy, she didn't realize that she shouldn't do that. She would go into our garden, extract the bark chips, chew them, and try to swallow them. Fortunately, we kept a close eye on her since she was a small puppy, and we would stop her before she swallowed something that might not feel good coming out the other end.

Dogs and humans may not always be aware of what is good for them. We do have the ability to know what is good for us; we may simply not be *aware* that we know. Consequently, in a state of unawareness, we ingest harmful things into our bodies and minds.

I'm referring not only to unhealthy foods and other harmful substances. I am also referring to negativity and other poisons that sabotage success. Unhealthy eating, over-indulgence in harmful beverages, and a negative attitude will all sabotage success.

When speaking to audiences, I often ask people, "If I put poison in your water would you drink it?" What do you suppose is the answer? Obviously, "no!"

Our bodies require good nutrition to survive, as does our mind. If we do not treat our body well, it will respond accordingly. We may think that one sugar-filled food or beverage a day isn't hurting us, until we add up the 365 that we ate or drank this year and calculate the possible damage. What happens when this type of eating or drinking pattern is repeated over several years? You can be sure there will be health-related challenges.

About 25 years ago I heard someone say, "Most people are digging their graves with their mouths." True as that statement is, my understanding is that not only is someone slowly digging their grave by eating harmful foods and drinking weakening beverages, but the negativity that is spoken from the mouth is also extremely damaging.

Here's a simple example of the impact of a negative thought: having a fleeting thought that we are not worthy or deserving is a critical element in sabotaging one's success.

The negative thoughts that you have today *will* affect your results of tomorrow. Everything you have in your life today is the result of what went into your mind in the past.

How do you choose to feed your body, your mind and even your soul? Are you eating and drinking nutritional foods every day? Do you drink enough water every day? There are numerous reports, studies and reference material discussing the effects of the foods we eat and the beverages we drink and their relationship to our moods.

My recommendation is to become nutritionally conscious and apply healthy eating habits to your daily life. Additionally, feed your mind every day with positive thoughts and speak positive words. And remember to feed your soul. You can do this by meditating or reading an inspiring book.

Practicing healthy habits and behaviors will develop a healthy mind, body and soul. You will need a healthy mind, body and soul to live the way you were meant to live, fully enjoying life at the highest level.

Chapter 5

Be a Little Dog with Big-Dog Attitude
Your attitude is the little thing that makes the big difference.

What counts is not necessarily the size of the dog in the fight; it's the size of the fight in the dog.
~ Dwight D. Eisenhower ~

What does it mean to be a little dog with big-dog attitude?

Little dogs don't realize that they are little; they act as if they are big dogs despite their size. They have no fear, and are not intimidated by other dogs regardless of the size. Small dogs will try to do things even bigger dogs might think are impossible. Small dogs don't know these things are impossible, so they try anyway. What a great attitude to walk around with – courageous and confident!

A positive attitude

Do you have a positive and optimistic attitude? If not, I strongly urge you to develop one immediately. You can quickly acquire a positive attitude by being consistently grateful. A grateful heart will produce a positive mind.

With a positive and optimistic attitude added to your determination to never let go of your dreams, you will reduce and possibly eliminate most negative feelings, such as frustration and stress.

Having an intense negative attitude, on the other hand, will stop you in your tracks and will send you in a backward direction at an accelerated rate. A negative attitude (feeling irritated by the weather, the economy or some other condition outside of your control) will infect all areas of your life unless you stop, consider the ramifications, and change your thinking.

A positive attitude has many fundamental and positive side effects. Life is far more enjoyable, you'll manage better through obstacles and challenges, you will strive and reach higher and you will attract to you all that you need in order to achieve your goals.

Ignore what others think about you

If you investigated the characteristics of some of the most successful people in the world, you'd find they give very little energy or concern to what others think of them.

Terry Cole Whittaker wrote a wonderful book on this subject called *What You Think of Me Is None of My Business*.

Do not be concerned with what others think of you or say about you, especially when they start to see the positive changes in your life. Change is sometimes difficult for people to adjust to, and when an individual starts to change for the better, those around them often respond negatively. Do not let this dissuade you. Maintain your positive attitude. Keep focused on your goal. Build your faith, and after they start to see your level of commitment and notice that the changes are positive, if they truly care for you, they will be happy for you.

Be confident

Quite often I hear owners of a Yorkshire Terrier tell me that their little dog has a big-dog attitude. The little terrier, fully grown, may weigh only 3 or 4 pounds, but it has no inhibitions when a large dog comes along. A Yorky will enthusiastically run up to a large dog and attempt to engage it in play.

The following story comes from Deneen. Deneen is a dog handler and trainer. She shares with us a story about her own dog Keaton who was enrolled in Agility training. Dog Agility is a dog sport that includes leaping over a variety of jumps, tipping a see-saw, zipping through a configuration of upright poles, negotiating a narrow dog-walk and zooming through tunnels.

"Can Do" Keaton

When I tell people that I do Agility with my dog they ask, "What breed is he?" and expect to hear Golden Retriever, Jack Russell or Border Collie. Well, it comes as quite a shock to them that Keaton is a 2-year-old, brindle and white English Bulldog.

That's when the negative comments start. "A Bulldog in Agility?" "Bulldogs can't do **that!**" "He could **never** jump or climb the A Frame!" and "Bulldogs are stubborn, stupid and not trainable!!"

The sad thing was, at first, I started to believe them too, but Keaton convinced me otherwise.

After Keaton's first beginner classes, it became very clear that the piece of equipment known as the "A Frame" was going to be a monumental challenge. With the A Frame at a peak of 5'6" high, this mountain of boards, with only small slats of wood for traction, started to look a lot like Mt. Everest!

On Keaton's first attempt, our goal was not the same as the other dogs' in the agility training. Our goal was to have Keaton place his front feet onto the frame. We accomplished our goal, and Keaton was rewarded to let him know that he had succeeded. Our next goal was to get all four feet on the frame at the same time. He did it! Another treat and words of encouragement for Keaton's accomplishment.

That was all for the first class. I couldn't help thinking, "Well, that went well, but it didn't seem to be much of an accomplishment compared to what the other dogs were doing."

The following week the pressure really seemed on. The other dogs were sailing up and over the frame on their first attempt. Keaton was still apprehensive and only willing to put a paw or two on the first step of the frame. "That's good enough for this class," the instructor stated. "We'll try for a little more next week."

And that's when more negativity crept into my head. "Maybe he can't do this . . . he is a Bulldog after all."

Feeling disappointed, I clipped on his lead and started to follow the others out of class. That's when Keaton let out a bark and started to pull me, with great determination, back in the direction of the A Frame. Before I could think, "You won't do this . . . you're a Bulldog," he picked up speed, confidently put his feet onto the yellow frame, and powered himself up and over that frame with great ease. Once he was down the other side he sauntered proudly towards the door as if to say, "So there! We can go home now."

It didn't matter that no one in the class had seen him do it. I was filled with inspiration at his confidence and determination. We were ready to show everyone what a Bulldog can do, and that is exactly what he did at the very next class.

Today, Keaton still loves training in Agility and Obedience and is preparing to compete for his Novice titles. He is a confirmation Champion. In his spare time, he plays the piano (yes, the piano) and we are working on a freestyle dance routine.

The lesson Keaton taught me

Keaton taught me to take those negative thoughts and opinions that others may have and that I have adopted, that have held me back from achieving my goals, and throw them away. He taught me to not worry about what everyone else is doing; to decide for myself and take it step by step. I learned to plan my strategy and I learned that I can climb any mountain.

Even if your situation isn't ideal and the circumstances aren't the most opportune, even if you don't believe that you can make huge leaps of advancement in a short period of time, pursue your dreams and goals anyway. You may have to place one paw out there at a time. Within a short period of time, you take another step and then another, until finally, you too are over the top.

Your attitude will make a big difference in your outcome. An optimistic attitude will turn the impossible into the possible.

Being positive and optimistic does not mean being arrogant. It is totally unattractive to see people running around being braggadocios, or shouting the strong beliefs that they have about themselves.

All attitudes are held within and they will be expressed externally. Other people will be able to determine what your attitude is with or without verbal communication.

Trust yourself

Achieving great success and accomplishments requires an attitude of faith, confidence and assuredness. Create a deep sense of knowing that you have infinite potential; have faith and believe in yourself. Develop the state of mind of a winner. Have a winner's attitude, knowing that you have already arrived where you truly desire to go. Walk around as if you are already there, feeling what it feels like to have accomplished your goals and live the life of your dreams, being the person you've always dreamed of and sharing the gifts with others.

> *The greatest pleasure of a dog is that you may make a fool of yourself with him, and not only will he not scold you, but he will make a fool of himself too.*
> *~ Samuel Butler ~*

45

Chapter 6

When You Feel You've Reached the End of Your Leash, Go Farther
How to handle adversity and overcome any challenge

Every dog has his day.
~ Miguel de Cervantes ~

The first day we brought Dee Dee home, I put on her brand new beautiful collar, clipped on the matching leash, and was ready to go for a wonderful morning stroll, just as I had seen so many of my neighbors do with their dogs. You may already know where this is going, but I truly had great expectations of enjoying a peaceful walk with my dog.

If you've ever attempted to take a new puppy for a walk, you'll know that they want nothing to do with a leash. They want total freedom. A puppy's interest is to run in any direction it wants. For the first few weeks, I experienced this whenever I tried to walk Dee Dee with her new leash. She, like other puppies, is looking for full freedom: sprints, dashes and running in circles. However, in most societies, dogs are not allowed to run free. We must train our puppies to use the leash.

This type of training is fairly easy. It involves training the dog to go only as far as the leash will allow. Otherwise, they choke themselves and it becomes very uncomfortable for the dog.

Limitations and Beliefs

We experience a similar result when we try to stretch beyond our present limitations. Our limitations may be those we have set on our own, or those that society has set; in either case, we follow them blindly.

These limitations result from our beliefs, which may have been created at a young age. Our parents may have told us "you can't do that" or "you'll hurt yourself," and at that precise moment a boundary was set. Or, you could say, the end of our leash was set. It is also quite possible that the length of that leash was shortened and shortened over the years out of fear. This fear resulted in an uncomfortable feeling whenever we started to step beyond our current comfort level.

My belief is that our natural state is to pursue ultimate freedom and act without limitations.

Limitations can certainly play a beneficial role in our life and can provide a method of restraint. We need to ascertain which role the limitation is representing, a safe warning or an anchor.

So, if your leash isn't long enough, know that you have choices. You can get a new leash – a longer one or an adjustable one. In other words, if an old belief is holding you back, get rid of it, extend it or get a different belief. Although the leash is limited in length, the length can be changed. And there's another option: Let go of the leash and run freely in the direction of your goals.

The length of a leash also represents our own self-limiting barriers. You may have heard someone say, or you may have said this yourself, "I can't take it any more. This is as far as I can go!" Those are clear statements of defeat or resolve, with an intention to no longer move forward.

In some cases, this may be the best solution. If a statement like "I can't take it any more" implies some kind of abuse, then I highly recommend not taking any more and sticking to that decision. However, where there is simply a defeatist attitude and no physical or psychological harm is occurring, I recommend that you go just a bit farther. You may be extremely close to getting the results that you want.

Pet stores sell leashes with adjustable lengths of rope: you push a button and the lead will release or retract. The first time I used this type of lead I thought of how similar it was to the way some people live their lives. They have chosen how far they will go, and even though there is an opportunity to go farther, they don't bother expanding their leash. When things get tight, they draw in. Occasionally, they may pull beyond the length of the rope in an attempt to reach something outside of their normal limits.

The length of the leash is similar to our beliefs. We will only attempt to go as far as we believe we can go, even though nothing really stops us from going farther. When we expand our beliefs, we expand our reach.

We may think we have "reached the end of our rope," but as Zelda says, "Just when you reach the end of your rope, someone moves it." If your rope has moved, go after it. Defeat is never an option for a dog with a bone.

Change your limits

Have you decided where your "rope" ends? Consider that question for a moment. What limits have you set on yourself? Are these holding you back from achieving your goals? What would happen if you chose to let go of these limitations?

We set our own limits. They are not determined by others. We decide when we have reached the end of our rope, or how long the rope is. Think about your own life and your beliefs. If you have ever uttered the words, "I can't do this any more!" or "I've had it!" maybe you just need to take a rest and rebuild your energy. You may feel as if you are at the end of your rope, but you could quite possibly only need a break. You may need to take time, reflect, notice what you are feeling, and become aware of what is holding you back. Once you take that break, you can then be ready to charge forward.

Build faith

If you are still looking for answers and feel as if you are at the end of your rope, engage some additional patience and start to build faith. Faith is a state of being, a feeling of inner knowing, a conviction that you will achieve your goal. Faith is energy, a mighty and powerful energy.

You will need faith to continue. Where do you get faith? It's inside you. Faith, like determination, is a feeling that you can choose to have or choose not to have. It's up to you.

You can build faith by using your imagination and creative thoughts to "act as if." Essentially you think about your ideal outcome and imagine what it will feel like to reach it. While you are imagining, as you fully engage your imagination, you will start to have the feeling. The feeling comes from an imagined experience, regardless of any physical evidence. Once you have imagined your desired outcome and know what that feels like, you can practice having that feeling of accomplishment. "Acting as if" takes practice and may seem uncomfortable at first. With repeated practice you'll get it, and the mere exercise of doing this will build your faith.

Start with a little bit of faith, notice what it feels like, and add more faith to it. Add a little more faith every day, until you reach a point of absolute certainty. Keep in mind that having faith will result in the unknown becoming known. In other words, when you have decided on an outcome, even though you don't know how you will achieve it, with faith the answers will be revealed to you. Trust in this powerful energy of faith. The results of having faith will simply astound you.

"First my ball rolled under the sofa, then my water dish was too warm, then the squeaker broke on my squeaky rubber pork chop. I've had a horrible day and I'm completely stressed out!!!"

Chapter 7

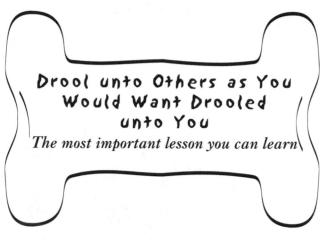

Drool unto Others as You Would Want Drooled unto You
The most important lesson you can learn

We are all one!

This is one of the most powerful and profound statements ever proclaimed.

Since we are all one, it is also true that what you do for another you do for yourself.

If you think that being nasty to one person isn't hurting you, I suggest you think again. There is a natural law of the universe which clearly states: What you put out you get back.

If you are putting out negativity, hostility, anger, resentment and any other negative emotion, it will be returned to you. Even a thought, negative or positive, will return similar energy to you.

Any time you think a negative or harmful thought, even if you don't speak the words, that thought has gone out into the universe as energy, pure energy in motion. It will be returned; there is no other way the universe knows how to respond.

My friend Mark Victor Hansen taught me to "be nice to everyone!" Not just some, but everyone. Become an unconditionally giving and loving person. Unconditionally means to be without an expectation of having that action or emotion returned.

If you are being unconditionally loving, love will be returned to you. If you are being respectful, respect will be returned to you. If you are being kind, kindness will be returned to you, and so on and so on. It may not be returned from the person that it was intended for; nonetheless, it will be returned.

> *The average dog is a nicer person than the average person.*
> *~ Andy Rooney~*

Without a doubt, dogs are unconditionally loving. Your dog will love you no matter what kind of day you are having. Even if you are sad, the dog is there to love you. When you are frustrated, depressed, drained, the dog is there to wag its tail and lick your face. Dogs do not determine how they will treat you based on your mood. They love you regardless of your mood. I think this is one of the reasons dog owners love their dogs so much. The dog loves the owner unconditionally and without judgment. Human relationships would improve significantly if human beings adopted the same high level of acceptance and love.

Most dog owners also love their dogs unconditionally – masters love their dogs without any expectation of love in return. But do humans love each other without conditions? Rarely. Why is that? Humans are afraid to love unconditionally because they are afraid of being hurt, rejected or disappointed. In general, dogs are not concerned with being hurt, rejected or disappointed. Do you think we could learn from this behavior? You bet we can.

The good you send out

When Dee Dee was a small puppy she would go everywhere with me; at least, wherever she would be welcomed. One day I had a meeting with Fernando Martinez, my web site designer. Fernando warmly and openly welcomed Dee Dee to our meetings. One day, as I was sitting in the reception area of Fernando's building, a gentleman walked out of one of the other offices and came up to see my little Dee Dee. She was an adorable puppy and attracted people to her like a magnet.

This gentleman didn't tell me his name but he did share his story about one of his dogs.

A few years earlier he had a Scottish Terrier and she was beautiful. They loved her very much. At the young age of 3, she died of cancer.

They missed their Scotty terribly. His wife convinced him to go to see the Kennel Dogs. There they saw another Scottish Terrier that nobody seemed to want. She was a very unattractive dog and was missing hair around one ear. This Scotty was 2 years old. They felt sorry for this dog and out of pity they gave her a home. A few years later they were very glad that they had done so. This little unattractive Scottish Terrier saved their lives one night when she woke them up at 2:00 am, as their house was on fire. Their Scotty saved their lives, just as they had saved hers.

Being nice to everyone and being unconditionally loving also means being respectful of others. Respect is a value that should be high on the values list.

There have been times in my career when I've experienced people treating me inappropriately. Later on, down the road, they came into my office looking for a job. How do you think I felt about that person at the time? Do you think their previous treatment had any effect on my decision to hire them? You just never know where people will show up in your life and, if for only this reason, being nice to everyone is very important.

If you pick up a starving dog and make him prosperous, he will not bite you. This is the principal difference between a dog and a man.
~ Mark Twain ~

Don't bite the hand that feeds you

When my two puppies were very young they would play-fully bite our fingers. My son Michel would teasingly say to them, "Don't bite the hand that feeds you."

The "hand that feeds you" may be your customers, your employer, your life partner, your children, your other family members, your friends, or strangers. The word "feed" could also be replaced by the word "love." The hand represents the whole person. And the word "bite" could be replaced by "be nasty to." So "Don't be nasty to the person who loves you."

In other words, be kind to everyone. The one clear message in this chapter is really quite simple: treat others as you would like to be treated yourself.

Don't accept your dog's admiration as conclusive evidence that you are wonderful.
~ Ann Landers ~

"Remember the Golden Rule: Drool unto others
as you would have them drool unto you!"

Chapter 8

Come on out of the Doghouse
*Courageously step forward
into growth.*

Is it really a "dog eat dog" world out there? Life can sometimes be "ruff" for some, while it is not for others. When life gets tough, don't cower away in the comfort of your doghouse. Come on out and face the world. Cowering will not solve anything. Cowering could, quite possibly, make things worse. Pretending that things aren't there does not make them go away. If you have something that you need to face, then face it head on.

When I was a young child and started to realize the tragedies and horrific events that occurred and were occurring in our world, I recall thinking to myself, "I don't want to grow up!" Life wasn't what I had imagined it to be. I imagined everyone had happy families, comfortable homes, plenty of food to eat, and clean clothes on their back. As a child I was sheltered from the world's tragedies and once I started to hear about them through the media, school or friends, I was shocked. Imagine . . . people were starving to death! How could that be?

I couldn't go back to being a younger child. My only choice was to get older, and getting older included becoming more aware of the realities of life, all of them. I quickly learned that life wasn't as easy for everyone as I had imagined it to be, and the same thing started to happen in my own life: I started to have increasingly more challenges. My response to all of this change was a desire to step back into comfort.

What can you do?

Life has one constant, and that one constant is change. Change is inevitable. Everything in the universe is changing. You know, as I do, that we don't have control over everything that is happening, but what we do have control over is the way we respond to what happens to us. Our response to what happens to us will determine our results.

If the change that is happening in your life is not a change that you have chosen, ignoring it will not help the matter. The change could be a blessing in disguise. There have been times in my own life when a dreaded or forced change resulted in one of the best growing and learning experiences of my life.

You choose how you will respond to events and what you will do about them. With a positive attitude and a courageous approach, you'll be able to manage through change more effectively. If the change is going to happen, or is happening anyway, you may as well make the best of it.

Impossible situations

Have you backed yourself into a corner?

Being backed into a corner is another way of saying there is no way out, resulting in a feeling of desperation. This may have occurred as the result of doing something that backfired on you, or experiencing an event that left you with what you believe to be no options.

You may also feel as if, having backed yourself into a corner, vicious animals are awaiting you. Is it possible that you can come out without provoking an attack on you? Perhaps the fear you face will disappear when you meet it head on. What if you came out of the corner and you were greeted with a wagging tail?

There is always a way to solve any dilemma. You must find a way to resolve the situation gracefully, if the situation needs to be resolved. Forgiveness may be a solution. You may need to learn from the experience and forgive yourself, and you may need to forgive another. Whatever is required, find a way.

You may have had an experience whereby someone caused you serious upset. The best approach, rather than retaliation, may be to just let the sleeping dog lie. The past is the past, and that is where it may need to be left, behind you.

Windows of opportunity

When you have decided to step courageously forward and you are now determined to achieve your goal, you will start to find windows of opportunity opening up for you. But you won't see them if you are not willing and ready to see them.

My neighbor's dog Holly will ask to go outside by walking up to the door and waiting patiently for Cheryl to open the door. When Cheryl opens the door for Holly, the dog will move to the side and sit down. Cheryl smiles as Holly just sits there . . . still inside. The door is open and Holly just looks at the door and then looks back up at Cheryl. Holly will wait until Cheryl is just about to close the door, and then she runs outside. Cheryl calls this Holly's Window of Opportunity. Holly always makes it.

This behavior reminds me of people who see the window of opportunity and don't do anything about it. Then, just as the window is about to close, they go for it.

But what about those people who have windows of opportunity open up for them and they don't do anything about it at all? Or, even worse, the windows of opportunity are there and they don't even see them?

Every day is a new opportunity. You've got to be ready to seize these opportunities. Sometimes the best opportunities are right under your nose. Or, if you don't have windows of opportunity, or you can't find them, create your own opportunities.

"Cats—the fragrance for dogs who dare to be different!"

Chapter 9

Dog Instincts
Trust your inner knowing.

*Outside of a dog, a book is probably man's best
friend; inside of a dog, it's too dark to read.*
~ Groucho Marx ~

Dogs have incredibly refined instincts. They can sense
danger – they will growl when they feel danger is near.
Their instincts tell them whether a human being is a
loving person or not. They also have a keen awareness of
when someone is ill or about to become gravely ill. Dogs
have a strong sense of instinct and they trust it. They
don't question it.

There are numerous stories of people who suffer from
epileptic seizures who have dogs that will notify them
prior to the onset of a seizure, so that they can place
themselves in a safe position and get the proper medica-
tion required.

One of the reasons for dogs' keen sense is that their ability to detect odor is perhaps a million times more acute than humans'. It is speculated that certain diseases, like cancer, epilepsy, tuberculosis and many other diseases, emit a distinctive odor that is recognizable to dogs.

My cousin Fern shared this story about Zeus, a 30-pound Schnauzer.

> *Zeus had cancer when I met him. He had a tumor the size of a tennis ball on his back leg. My dog, Duchess, a German Shepherd, as well as other dogs, instinctively knew not to play with him, to respect him and his illness. It amazed me to see that the dogs had such an intuitive knowing not to disturb Zeus. Zeus's owner took Zeus to Boston for cancer treatment.*
>
> *When Zeus and his owner returned, Zeus appeared to be healthy again. He was no longer limping and, in fact, he was running around again. The dogs began to play with him, include him, and rough-house with him. Nine months later, the dogs began to leave him alone again, even though he appeared to be fine. Zeus's owner noticed that the other dogs were no longer playing with him or including him and decided to take him to the veterinarian. The vet diagnosed that Zeus's cancer had returned, and the dog died shortly thereafter.*

Because of the dogs' keen sense, they were able to detect Zeus's health issues even before the owner did. A dog's instinct for danger and sickness is so refined that it can detect when another dog or person is sick before they have been diagnosed by a medical professional.

A similar story was shared by my Aunt Betty. She told me a story about her cousin Neil's dog. Betty's Aunt Jessie had a son, Neil, who was a wireless air-gunner for the Royal Canadian Air Force during World War II. Neil had a dog he was very attached to, which he left with his mother Jessie while he was overseas fighting in the war. One night, in the middle of the night, Neil's dog woke up and started to howl for no apparent reason. He howled for hours, and no matter what Jessie did, she could not settle the dog down. Within a few days the R.C.A.F. notified Jessie that her son Neil was presumed dead. Neil had gone missing a few nights earlier when he did not return from his mission.

How did Neil's dog know that he was killed on that particular night, when they were thousands of miles apart and an ocean separated them? The only answer is: a dog's instincts.

Randy Chartrand is a psychological expert on dogs. He is one of the best dog trainers in the country. Randy says: "Dogs are emotional. Fear is an emotion that will save a dog's life. Fear is a survival emotion. Sometimes it is better for a dog to take off when they sense danger, and they will do just that."

Humans are emotional as well. Humans can detect danger, and will feel the fear. However, humans have so many destructive, self-induced emotions that clutter their instinctual senses that they become confused.

One of the best things that a human can do to get in touch with his or her instincts is to become quiet and listen to their inner voice. The inner voice is the inner knowing. Your instincts will reveal to you valuable information. If your instinct is fear-based, you can evaluate whether the fear is based on reality or imagination. Most of the time fear is based upon an imagined result, a fear of what could occur, rather than on what actually occurs.

Just as with dogs, fear can be a survival emotion. When you feel fear, get in touch with that emotion, and determine the cause. If there is validity to the fear, determine your course of action.

Most importantly, take the necessary action. If you need to, do as a dog would do and take off when you sense danger. Or, if the fear is only imagined, step forward in spite of the fear and quite likely it will disappear.

> *It is funny how dogs and cats know the inside of folks better than other folks do.*
> *~ Eleanor H. Porter, "Pollyanna," 1912 ~*

Learn to trust your instincts. Instincts can be the greatest barometer you have. Once you begin to trust your instincts you'll be able to easily determine if a certain feeling is coming from your inner knowing or from false evidence that only appears to be real. If you want to know what your instincts are communicating to you do the *tummy test*. What is your tummy telling you about a particular situation? Is it fluttering or is it calm? Your tummy never lies.

When you learn to listen and trust your instincts, you will begin to build keener senses. With your keen instincts you too will be better equipped to "sniff for trouble" and avoid it, and make decisions based on an accurate reading of the situation.

Chapter 10

Bark for What You Want
Ask for what you want.

**"The microphone is so you can go to
Internet chat rooms and bark at strangers."**

Jack Canfield taught me many years ago to ask for what I want. He said if there is something that you want, ask, ask, ask. Just like our little Dee Dee, who will walk over to you, lie down on her back and look at you as if to say "please rub my tummy," Dee Dee will lie trustingly on her back, look at you with her big brown eyes, and wait confidently for you to rub her tummy.

Does a dog think twice before it asks for what it wants? Dogs will ask to be let outside; they'll ask to be fed; they'll ask you to play ball. They'll look up at you with those puppy-dog eyes and you are doomed. They don't think about it, or analyze it; they just do it. They are not even afraid of the answer. If the answer is "no," they'll keep asking.

Humans need to remember to ask for what we want, appropriately and respectfully. You may want to consider using your puppy-dog eyes to ask.

> *If dogs could talk it would take a lot of fun out of*
> *owning one.*
> ~ *Andy Rooney* ~

People will help you

Early in my writing career I learned that people do want to help you, but how will people know that you need help unless you ask? I also believe that people want to help others, who in turn want to help others. This creates a chain reaction of giving.

Why is it that people are more reluctant to ask a friend for a favor than they are a stranger? People don't ask their friends because they are concerned that it will jeopardize the friendship. If we can't do things for our friends, for whom can we do them? A true friend loves to help out another friend. It is a privilege to help.

Be open to receiving help when it is offered to you. Most people love to help. It gives people pleasure to be able to help. Accept the help and you will, in turn, be giving a gift to the person who is helping.

There may be times when you are on the receiving end of a request. When you are the one who is being asked to help, accept the request. Help others in any way that you can. Don't wait to be asked for help. If you see someone struggling and you know you can help, do it. Give without expectation of anything in return; otherwise you may only set yourself up for disappointment.

Barking and biting

If you do come across an individual who is using a harsh tone to make a request, remember their bark is probably worse than their bite. However, making demands does not achieve great results. Demands are not well accepted, nor do they always get the desired results, and they usually lead to greater challenges down the road.

> *The silent dog is the first to bite.*
> ~ *German Proverb* ~

The best approach to making a request is to do so with sincerity, honesty and openness. Be clear on what it is that you want, and ask. Don't be intimidated or fearful of a negative response. Your emotions will come through in your request and if you are timid about the request, the person who is receiving the request will feel your discomfort and may feel uncomfortable about responding. Be confident and assured when making your request. What is the worse that can happen? They say "no" and, if they do, you haven't lost a thing.

When do you stop asking? When you get the answers or the results you want. Keep asking until you get what you want. The law of averages will work for you. You may not get a favorable response on your first request, so keep asking until you do.

Bark for what you want, but bark gently, respectfully, and do it with those big puppy-dog eyes. You will be irresistible.

Chapter 11

Wag Your Tail
Be happy and show appreciation.

"This is so cool! I'm barking at a cat in Australia!"

How often do we express our gratitude and appreciation to others? Do you wag your tail when your partner arrives home? Too often we feel grateful to another and appreciative, but we are reluctant to express it.

Dogs show appreciation all the time. Dogs will show appreciation just for you showing up. Have you ever been greeted by your dog when you have been out for a while? They have a greeting that says "I'm so glad you are here." Dogs will show their appreciation even if you have only been out for 5 minutes.

> *To his dog, every man is Napoleon; hence the constant popularity of dogs.*
> ~ *Aldous Huxley* ~

How often have you returned home from work and found your other family members so busy that they haven't even noticed you entered the premises? But the dog has given you a warm reception, licking you, wagging its tail and possibly jumping up with enthusiasm, excited just by your presence.

A two-way gift

Showing appreciation to others benefits them *and* you. Have you ever noticed that when you show appreciation to another you make them feel good? How does that make you feel? It makes you feel good too. That is why this expression is true: it is better to give than to receive.

> *Pet a dog where he can't scratch and he'll always be your friend.*
> ~ *Orville Mars* ~

You can give a gift to another by expressing your appreciation. The appreciation could be for something as simple as who they are, or a special thing that they have done for you.

Being appreciated is the same thing as having someone tell you that they care for you. Appreciation communicates respect, admiration, thankfulness, gratitude and love. Everyone loves to be appreciated. Since you know how good it feels to receive, find ways by which you can show your appreciation to your family members, your customers, your co-workers, your employer, your neighbors, your friends and even strangers.

> *You call to a dog and a dog will break its neck to get to you. Dogs just want to please. Call to a cat and its attitude is, "What's in it for me?"*
> *~ Lewis Grizzard ~*

Acknowledge good behavior

Dogs and humans crave attention and emotion, any emotion. When a human is feeling neglected, he or she will, instinctively, do something to gain attention. The thing they "do" is not always a positive action. Dogs are the same. If a dog is being ignored, he will find a way to get attention.

In puppy training, dog owners are taught to praise the pups when they do something that they are being trained to do. Why? Because this reinforces the behavior of the puppy and it will repeat the behavior when it is rewarded.

This principle of acknowledging good behavior works with humans too. Praise others when they display positive behavior ("good boy" or "good girl") and you will see this behavior repeated.

Dogs and the prevention of illness

According to medical professionals, owning a dog will reduce your risk of heart-related illnesses, such as heart disease. It is also proven that owning a dog will lower blood pressure and reduce high cholesterol. The *Journal of Personality and Social Psychology* published a report that stated that dog owners require less medical attention and have up to 21 percent fewer visits to their doctor.

The same is true for dogs. When a dog is petted, stroked, cuddled and lovingly cared for, its heart rate and blood pressure are also significantly reduced.

Studies have also proven that elderly people live longer when they own a pet, such as a dog. Why? The answer is fairly obvious. First, they have someone that needs their care, and second, they too are loved and appreciated by their pet.

Wag your tail every day

Expressing your gratitude and appreciation to others will increase your level of happiness. When you feel good you express joy. When you express joy you feel good. It is a circle. Not a vicious circle, but a circle of love. Giving unconditional thanks and appreciation is a loving gesture that will release the powerful energy of love and it will be returned to you multiplied. Imagine what your life would be like then! Start today and find someone, or many people, to whom you can express your genuine appreciation and gratitude.

"My therapy is quite simple: I wag my tail and lick your face until you feel good about yourself again."

Chapter 12

Keep Your Nose Wet
What to do when you are feeling ruff

A dog is the only thing on earth that loves you more than you love yourself.
~ Josh Billings ~

Have you ever witnessed someone push themselves way beyond their physical limitations? How can someone enjoy success when they sacrifice their health to get it?

Working like a dog and ignoring the importance of health will certainly lead to health-related challenges. Preventive maintenance, as it relates to health, should be a high priority in everyone's life. Creating phenomenal success is of no value if you are not healthy enough to enjoy it. It amazes me when people invest so much of themselves – time, energy and money – to become successful, sacrificing the very thing that will allow them to enjoy this new level of achievement: their health and well-being.

Take care of yourself

Are you taking great care of yourself? What do you do to stay healthy? What do you do to return to health when you are not feeling well?

You must take care of your physical body and your mind. Why? Your body and your mind are the vehicles that will carry you to your goals.

You will know when you haven't been taking care of yourself, as the results will be revealed to you in time. When a dog's nose is wet and cool, it usually means the dog is healthy. A dog's nose is the health indicator of the dog for a dog owner. If a dog's nose is dry and warm, it usually means there is something wrong and attention is required. With a dog, it is sometimes difficult to determine in advance whether it has any health issues. With humans, we have the ability to determine potential health challenges much sooner. Notice when you start to feel unhealthy effects of working too hard, and adjust before you create a greater health risk.

Your attitude affects your health

While you are striving to reach your goals, there may be days when you do not feel the best. You will need to turn up the intensity on your positive attitude on days like this and maybe even exert a little more energy, in small doses, when you need to.

"A professional is at their best regardless." This statement simply means that, even though we may not always feel the greatest, we should always perform at the best of our ability in the moment.

Take time to play

Playtime is good for the mind, the body and the soul. Make sure that you have a balance of work and play. Dogs take time to play; they never forget to play. But sometimes humans do, especially when they are behaving like a dog with a bone. Focusing on your dreams like a dog with a bone does *not* mean you should refuse to take time for play. Play is an important part of having life balance. Dogs make it part of their every day.

Are you a worrier?

Dogs don't appear to worry. Maybe this characteristic is not built into dogs, and luckily for them, they also don't have the painful side effects. Many adult human beings, on the other hand, do have a tendency to worry. But worry is an emotion that can cause intense pain and self-destruction. Worry can also be an emotion that could be replaced with caution. Instead of worrying, be cautious or curious.

Shake off the negativity

When a dog gets out of the water it shakes its body to get rid of the water on its coat. What if you used this action as a metaphor for what to do when you are feeling an increased level of negativity such as stress, anger, frustration? Shake it off. Negativity has no purpose in your life and needs to be removed immediately.

Don't push yourself too far

Dogs, like humans, have been known to push themselves beyond their physical limits. As you may recall, we introduced Max the Scotty in Chapter 1. David continues his story about Max:

When we lived in Boston, two girls from the neighborhood would take our two dogs out and walk them and play with them. This would give the dogs exercise. The two little girls would have the dogs chase the ball across the floor in their basement. They would do this until Max's paws bled. Max's paws would be bleeding and he would still go back for more. Max was determined to keep going in spite of physical pain.

Max was the dog with the dogged determination to play with the ball. Although we can learn from Max's example in his determination to play, we can also learn from his example in enduring physical pain. Was it necessary for Max to play so hard that his paws bled? No! His level of determination was so fixated that he went beyond his physical limits.

Having determination does not mean that we go beyond our physical limits and endure physical pain. We need to remember not to push ourselves too far. Working long hours, not eating properly, not drinking enough water, not exercising – these are all examples of things that we need to notice if our determination has gone over the limit.

Max's story teaches us to recognize when we have exceeded our physical limits, so that we can stop and take care of our physical body.

Practice proper grooming

Take regular trips to the "groomer" and keep up a professional appearance. A large part of success is relationships, and building relationships starts with a first impression. Your appearance is the criterion by which an impression will be made. People will judge you based on how you look even before you have opened your mouth. Make your image an important part of your priorities, and dress for success.

> *No one appreciates the very special genius of your conversation as a dog does.*
> *~ Christopher Morley ~*

Chapter 13

The Dogma of Success
The Inside Scoop
to live your life by

"Don't worry—I'm just practicing my Yoga!"

There are those who work like a dog to make things happen, there are those who watch things happen, and then there are those who wonder what happened. Be the person who makes things happen.

Sometimes you have to work like a dog. If you want to be extraordinary, you must do the things that ordinary people are not willing to do. Success does not occur through merely wishing for success. But it also doesn't occur through force. Trying to force success to happen, or getting incredibly frustrated when things are not happening exactly the way you would like, demonstrates an unawareness of the perfection of the universe.

All things are happening for a reason, and if you attempt to understand why everything is happening as it's happening, or understand why things have happened the way they have, you may meet with frustration. Sometimes it is necessary to "let go" or, as it has been said, "let go and let God." But letting go and letting God does not mean that you can sit back and wish for things to happen and not do anything about it. On the contrary, you do have a responsibility for what is going to show up for you in your life.

Creating success in your life is aligning all of the factors for success in a fashion that will produce your desired results, not the results someone else desired for you, but what you truly desire for yourself.

What are those factors? Depending on the outcome you are seeking, you'll create your own formula based on what you want to produce. There are, however, some fundamental ingredients that will be required, such as: passion, integrity, determination, focus, optimism, faith, a positive attitude, awareness, decision, commitment and love.

There is no single dog training program that will work for all dogs, just as there isn't one that will work for all humans. All dogs and all humans are unique.

What brings out the best in your dog is an understanding of your dog's individuality. The same applies to humans. For you to bring out the best in you, you need to understand yourself. Make it a study to really understand yourself: your behaviors, your habits, your areas of focus, your daily rituals, your choices and your unique talents. Become acutely aware of what you are creating in your life and discover the methods of turning your talents into the strengths that will in turn transform your goals into concrete manifestations.

If you want to be successful, find someone who is already successful and follow them around like a puppy dog. Success breeds success. Modeling another person's success will significantly reduce your time to reach success. Why? These "models" have already been there. They have learned the lessons. They have learned what to do and, more importantly, what not to do. Follow their example, but make it your own. Don't be a copy cat. Enhance your own success by customizing the success techniques of another to suit your goals. Once you have done that, look for ways to improve these techniques for yourself.

In my own business I have used this technique. When I launched my first online e-mail campaign I found the people who were getting the results that I wanted. I asked them how they achieved their success. I listened intently and noted the things they did that were "results-producing" and the things they did that were "learning experiences." I adapted their experience to my plan, eliminating the costly mistakes and creating ways to improve the campaigns to generate increased sales for my own business.

Unlimited potential

Just like dogs, we humans are far more capable than we currently appear. Do you realize that service dogs can do things such as turn on lights, push buttons, pull books out of backpacks, get pens out, help with wheelchair lifts, etc.? These dogs are trained to do these things. Until I started doing more in-depth study on dogs I had no idea that dogs were capable of performing all of these actions.

We too can do the impossible. The only thing that stops us is our limiting beliefs about our own abilities. If we believe we will not be able to do a certain thing, then we will see the manifestation of that belief. However, if we choose to adopt the philosophy of "there is a way" and "I will find it," then we move beyond the impossible to the possible.

You've got the ability to do anything you want with your life. Know that. Trust it and be committed to your goals and don't let anyone or anything stand in your way or try to take your dreams away from you.

Be clear about your dream. Then, be the dog with a bone, have faith, and know in your heart that it will manifest!

And, as Winston Churchill used to say: *"Never, ever, ever give up"* on your dreams.

Chapter 14

Lap up Your Success
Take a bite out of life.

Just give me a comfortable couch, a dog, a good book, and a woman. Then if you can get the dog to go somewhere and read the book, I might have a little fun!
~ Groucho Marx ~

Paws (pause) for a moment and give thanks for the many blessings in your life. Paws and take inventory of the great gifts you have been given, and are about to receive. Give thanks for the gifts that you share with others. Gratitude will create a wondrous feeling of joy.

Remember, as you are on your journey to success, enjoy the trip. Stick your head out of the car window, just like a dog does, and let the wind blow through your hair.

This journey requires your commitment. Success is a commitment. The successful people that you know have chosen to be successful. Choose success. You are evolving and transforming continuously. Decide how you will grow and make positive progress every day in every way.

Once you've got that dog with a bone attitude, keep it. Hang on to that bone and don't let impolite people or unaware people try to take it away from you. Remind yourself of what keeps your jaws clenched on that bone (your dream). This is your inspiration. This is your fire. This is the one thing that will drive you to keep hold of the bone.

The universe lines up to provide for a person who is a dog with a bone. This is where the miracles start to happen and the "serendipitous" moments occur.

Here you'll discover the resources and methods for lapping up your success and fully enjoying your life.

And don't forget to give yourself a "treat" when you have accomplished a goal, or even one step toward the achievement of a goal! Dog owners give their dogs treats when they do good things; you should at least do the same for yourself.

"We'd like tonight to be special.
Could you get some water from the toilet
and put it in a champagne bottle?"

Finally, celebrate! Celebrate your life, your learning, your every success. Celebrate your accomplishments big or small. And celebrate the success of your friends, your colleagues and your family. Enjoy the wonderful and exciting journey. Unlike cats, we have only one life to live, so live it to its fullest. Take a bite out of life and savor every mouth-watering moment.

Profile of Zelda

Zelda is a six year old supermodel English bulldog whose endearing images have captured millions of hearts worldwide. Her lovable mug has launched the international Zelda Wisdom merchandising line including greeting cards, books, calendars, stationary products, figurines and posters. Tough but tender, sweet but strong, Zelda has attitude. Zelda Wisdom is a reflection of our hearts and souls; she allows us to laugh at ourselves and helps us realize that in life's ups and down, we are never alone. There is a Zelda in all of us! Zelda was recently named the official "spokesdog" for the Delta Society Pet Partners®, an international program dedicated to the human-animal healing bond.

Profile of Charlie

(The bulldog featured on the cover of this book.)

Canada's #1 Bulldog - 2002
Multi Best In Show Champion Rosehall's Good Time Charlie
From the very first moment we laid eyes on our new-born baby boy, we knew he was going places. His "got to love me!" attitude, accompanied with his textbook bully shuffle, won the hearts of judges and bulldog fanciers everywhere.

Charlie had achieved more awards before the age of 2 than many dogs achieve in their lifetime. Charlie comes from a long line of champions and top Canadian record-breaking bulldogs.

Words escape us.... pride and appreciation overwhelm us. We are truly blessed.
Robert and Elizabeth Bennett
Bulldogs of Rosehall

Endorsements

"This book is sure to be a classic. It's fast. . . . It's simple. . . It works! Peggy McColl will show you precisely what to do to hold on to your dreams AND to turn them into reality!"
— Bob Proctor, Author of the Best-Selling book *You Were Born Rich*

"This insightful book cleverly delivers a profound and meaningful approach on how you can turn your deepest desires into reality and transform your life."
— Mark Victor Hansen, Co-creator, #1 New York Times best-selling series *Chicken Soup for the Soul®*, Co-Author, *The One Minute Millionaire*

"A genuine masterpiece that reveals the true secrets to wisdom, success and fulfillment from the creatures who are most qualified to teach them to us . . . dogs."
— Dr. Paul Hartunian, Publicity Expert, www.Hartunian.com

"I love it! It's charming and wise, playful and brilliant, easy yet profound."
— Joe Vitale, #1 Best-Selling Author, *Spiritual Marketing*
http://www.mrfire.com

"Peggy's book offers fun and positive insights into the power of animals to teach us and enrich our lives. Her 'doggy' lessons instruct about serious life changes, while her stories and cartoons bring smiles, reminding us of the antics of our own four-footed family members."
— Linda M. Hines, Delta Society President/CEO, www.deltasociety.org

"When we asked our dog Roxy for her comment for this wonderful book she raised her head, offered that beautiful paw, and smiled 'Rorror!' Translating, I believe she said, 'Charming!'"
—Dottie Walters, *Author Speak & Grow Rich*

About the Author

Other titles available by Peggy McColl
On Being...The Creator of Your Destiny
ISBN 0-9730431-0-5

The 8 Proven Secrets to SMART Success
ISBN 0-9730431-2-1

Peggy McColl has been a featured speaker throughout Canada and the United States. Whether as a keynote conference speaker or booked for a corporation seminar, Peggy combines a depth of knowledge of her material with an unparalleled level of enthusiasm.

Peggy McColl gives power-seeking people the proven framework to define and conquer their goals, then recognize and reach their maximum potential.

Author of the phenomenally selling books *On Being . . . The Creator of Your Destiny*, *The 8 Proven Secrets to SMART Success* and *On Being a Dog with a Bone*, sold and distributed in over 26 countries in the world. Peggy is also the Founder and President of Dynamic Destinies Inc., where she has developed the powerful Goal Management Achievement Planning System (GoalMAPS) – the most compelling and strategic goal system of its kind.